Historical Biographies

# HATSHEPSUT

## First Female Pharaoh

## Peggy Pancella

Heinemann Library
Chicago, Illinois

© 2004 Heinemann Library
a division of Reed Elsevier Inc.
Chicago, Illinois

Customer Service  888-454-2279
Visit our website at www.heinemannlibrary.com

Designed by Lisa Buckley
Maps by John Fleck
Photo research by Julie Laffin
Printed and Bound in the United States by Lake Book Manufacturing, Inc.

08 07 06 05 04
10 9 8 7 6 5 4 3 2 1

**Library of Congress Cataloging-in-Publication Data**
Pancella, Peggy.
  Hatshepsut / Peggy Pancella.
     p. cm. -- (Historical biographies)
Summary: Presents an overview of Hatshepsut's life as well as her influence on history and the world.
Includes bibliographical references and index.
  ISBN 1-4034-3701-7 (HC), 1-4034-3709-2 (pbk.)
 1.  Hatshepsut, Queen of Egypt--Juvenile literature. 2. Pharaohs--Biography--Juvenile literature. [1. Hatshepsut, Queen of Egypt. 2. Kings, queens, rulers, etc. 3. Women--Biography. 4. Egypt--Civilization--To 332 B.C.] I. Title. II. Series.
  DT87.15.P37 2003
  932'.014--dc21
                         2003005919

**Acknowledgments**
The author and publisher are grateful to the following for permission to reproduce copyright material: Icon, pp. 4, 8, 16, 18 Erich Lessing/Art Resource, NY; p. 6 Gianni Dagli Orti/Corbis; pp. 7, 15, 17, 19, 22, 24, 26, 27 Ancient Art & Architecture Collection LTD; pp. 9, 11, 13, 14, 20, 21 Robert Harding Picture Library; pp. 10, 29 Heritage Image Partnership/The Image Works; pp. 12, 23 The Granger Collection; p. 28 Archivo Iconografico, S.A./Corbis.

Cover photograph: Sandro Vannini/Corbis, (background) Erich Lessing/Art Resource, NY

Special thanks to Michelle Rimsa for her comments in the preparation of this book.

Some words are shown in bold, **like this.** You can find out what they mean by looking in the glossary.

Many Egyptian names and terms may be found in the pronunciation guide.

The cover of this book shows a sculpture of Hatshepsut's face that was made in about 1498–1483 B.C.E.

# Contents

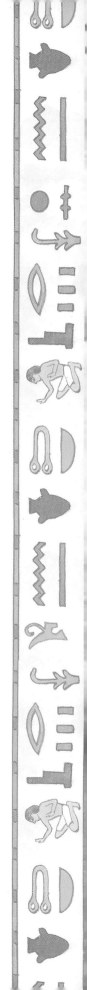

# Who Was Hatshepsut?

Hatshepsut lived long ago in Egypt. In ancient Egypt, powerful **pharaohs** ruled the land. Hatshepsut was born into a royal family and raised to be a queen. But she wanted more than that. Hatshepsut eventually became a pharaoh even though she was a woman.

### The world in Hatshepsut's time

During Hatshepsut's lifetime, many countries competed for power. Rulers wanted to control more land and people. They fought battles with other countries. The country that won could take over the other country and add it to its **empire**.

In about 3100 B.C.E., a king named Menes combined two areas called Upper Egypt and Lower Egypt. He was the first pharaoh. By the time Hatshepsut was born in about 1500 B.C.E., Egypt had defeated many other countries. Its empire stretched from present-day Sudan to the Euphrates River in Syria.

### How do we know about Hatshepsut?

Some information about Hatshepsut and ancient Egypt comes from writings people left behind.

▶ This is a statue of Hatshepsut. She proved that women could be just as good at leading as men were.

4

Archaeologists have also found many artifacts, such as statues, dishes, and jewelry, in Egypt. In addition, they have studied buildings, tombs, and ruins that remain. Archaeologists can learn who built buildings and how they were used. Many of the buildings have writing and pictures carved into them. Few images of Hatshepsut survive, but other clues help us to know about her life.

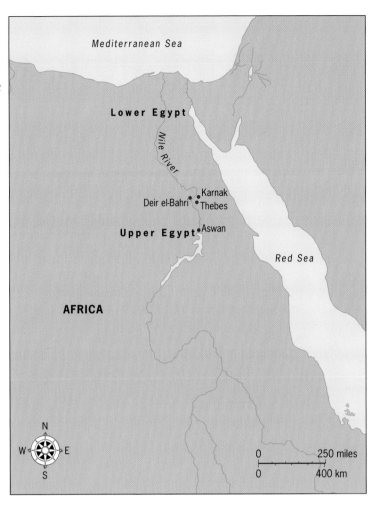

▲ This map shows some of the areas where archaeologists have found artifacts that have helped them learn about Hatshepsut.

### Key dates

| | |
|---|---|
| 1504–1492 B.C.E. | Tuthmosis I rules Egypt |
| about 1500 B.C.E. | Birth of Hatshepsut |
| 1492–1479 B.C.E. | Tuthmosis II rules Egypt |
| 1479–1473 B.C.E. | Hatshepsut serves as **regent** for Tuthmosis III |
| 1473–1458 B.C.E. | Hatshepsut rules Egypt as pharaoh |
| 1458–1425 B.C.E. | Tuthmosis III rules alone |

### Watch the dates

B.C.E. after a year means "before the common era." This is used instead of the older abbreviation B.C. The years are counted backwards toward zero. Historians are not sure about some dates of Hatshepsut's life. You may see different dates in different books.

# Life Along the Nile

Much of Egypt was desert land, so most people lived in a small area along the Nile River—the longest river in the world. The Nile provided fish to eat and water to drink.

Perhaps more important, the river flooded each year, carrying mud onto the farm fields. This mud made the farm fields good for growing crops.

### Work in Egypt

Most Egyptians were farmers. However, they could not farm when the fields flooded each year. Instead, some dug ditches and worked on the **pharaoh's** building projects. Other Egyptian workers were artists, **priests**, and soldiers. One of the most important jobs was that of a **scribe.** Unlike most Egyptians, scribes could read and write. They wrote letters and kept records for people.

▲ Egyptians did many types of work. Men are shown gathering grapes in this Egyptian wall painting from about 1400 B.C.E.

Boys from wealthy or **noble** families could go to school. They usually learned to do the same work as their fathers. Some girls were weavers, dancers, or musicians. Most stayed home to take care of the house and family. Even Hatshepsut had to learn how to run a household.

## Daily life

Egyptians lived in different types of houses. A noble family like Hatshepsut's probably had a large palace with many rooms and beautiful decorations. Poor farming families often had just one small room where they ate, worked, and slept.

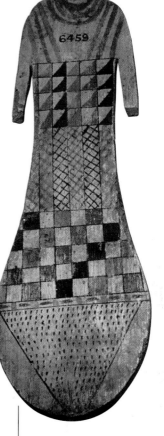

Because Egypt is so hot for much of the year, people did not wear many clothes. In fact, young children did not wear anything at all. Poor people wore simple clothes made of plain, rough cloth. Rich and powerful people like Hatshepsut's family had fine **linen** clothes and wore colorful jewelry. Men usually had short hair or shaved heads, while women had long hair or wore wigs. Egyptians also used lots of makeup, especially around their eyes.

▲ Some Egyptian children played with simple dolls like this one. It was made in about 1900 B.C.E.

## Fun and games

Egyptians worked hard, but they also made time for fun. Adults enjoyed hunting, sailing boats, racing **chariots,** and throwing dinner parties. Children played leapfrog and tug-of-war. They also had many toys, such as balls, tops, marbles, and dolls.

7

# A Pharaoh's Daughter

No one knows exactly when Hatshepsut was born. It was probably in about 1500 B.C.E. Her father was the **pharaoh** Tuthmosis I, and her mother was Queen Ahmose.

### Royal and divine

As pharaoh, Hatshepsut's father was a very powerful man. Some people thought he was like a god. He was allowed to have several wives, but Hatshepsut's mother was his favorite wife, or "God's Wife." She came from a royal family, too. The children they had together were considered both royal and **divine.**

Hatshepsut probably had many brothers and sisters. **Historians** know she had an older sister named Neferubity and two brothers named Wadjmose and Amenmose. The boys were not fully royal, like Hatshepsut, because their mothers were not from royal families. However, they were next in line to be pharaohs because they were boys.

### Hatshepsut's childhood

As the pharaoh's daughter, Hatshepsut lived in a fine palace and had everything she needed.

◄ This is a statue of Tuthmosis I, Hatshepsut's father.

Hatshepsut was especially close to her father. He took her along on some of his journeys and let her help with the day-to-day running of the **empire.** Unlike most girls of the time, Hatshepsut studied math, history, and religion, and learned to read and write.

In Hatshepsut's time, many children did not live long. No one knew how to cure most illnesses. One by one, Neferubity, Wadjmose, and Amenmose died. Hatshepsut was the only fully royal child left. She would have to help rule after her father.

▼ **Egyptian men usually wore kilts, while women wore dresses, as seen in this Egyptian wall painting.**

### Hatshepsut as a girl

Hatshepsut's father let her do many activities that girls of the time were not allowed to try. She enjoyed hunting trips and playing games that were usually only for boys. When she was young, she even dressed as a boy, wearing a short **kilt** instead of a dress. This behavior was unusual, but no one dared to tell the pharaoh that he should not allow it.

# In Her Father's Footsteps

Hatshepsut was still a child when her brothers and sister died. From that time, her life changed. Now she had to learn more about her land and how to run it. It was time to prepare herself to help rule someday.

## On the throne of Egypt?

When he was an old man, King Tuthmosis I died. The next **pharaoh** was already chosen—Tuthmosis II. He was Hatshepsut's half brother and a son of one of Tuthmosis I's other wives.

## Tuthmosis II and Hatshepsut

There was only one problem with Tuthmosis II—he was not fully royal. Ancient Egyptians believed that it was very important that their rulers have royal blood. Since Tuthmosis II was only half royal, he could only make things right by marrying someone who was fully royal. At the time, it was common for brothers and sisters and other relatives in royal families to marry each other. This was a way to keep a royal family going. So, Tuthmosis II married Hatshepsut.

▶ This statue shows Queen Ahmose, Hatshepsut's mother.

Hatshepsut received several new titles when she married, including the very important one of "God's Wife." She made herself busy with running the household. Hatshepsut and Tuthmosis II had one child, a girl named Neferure. Their life together was peaceful—at least for a while. After a short time, Tuthmosis II died. He had always had many problems with his health. Hatshepsut was alone again.

▶ This statue shows an Egyptian couple dressed for their wedding. The statue was found in a **tomb**.

### Marriage customs

In ancient Egypt, people married when they were twelve to sixteen years old. Some people chose their own husbands and wives, but parents arranged most marriages. Most nonroyal husbands had only one wife. Royal men like Tuthmosis I could have several wives. He did this to make sure he would have a son to rule after him. However, wives were never allowed to have more than one husband.

# Religious Beliefs

Ancient Egyptians believed in many gods and goddesses. Each god had special powers or could help in certain ways. There were gods for things in nature, such as the sun, water, and animals. Some gods helped certain groups of people, such as artists, travelers, or kings. There were also gods of music, dance, law, love, and even of the dead.

Sometimes there were special religious **festivals** that honored the gods. Festivals could also celebrate births, deaths, and the crowning of new **pharaohs**. Harvesttime, the changing of the seasons, and other special days were times to celebrate.

## *Worshiping the gods*

Egypt had many **temples** built to honor various gods. People could visit temples to offer gifts or pray to the gods. Many families also had small **shrines** inside their own homes. Children were taught about gods starting when they were young. As a child, Hatshepsut would have learned how to say prayers to the gods.

▲ The powerful Egyptian god Re is shown above crowned with the sun.

## Gods and the afterlife

The Egyptians believed that gods and goddesses could die and be reborn. When the gods died, they were thought to be in a perfect place called the Underworld. The Egyptians hoped that when they died, they could be with the gods in this perfect world.

The Egyptians preserved their bodies so they could enjoy the afterlife—a life existence after death. **Embalmers** treated dead bodies with chemicals to stop the bodies from decaying, or breaking down over time. They wrapped bodies in **linen** strips to create mummies. Some people were buried with *shabtis,* small statues they thought would turn into servants after death. **Tombs** could also include food, clothing, riches, and other objects the person might need.

▼ A mummy was buried in a coffin or in a larger, fancier container called a **sarcophagus** such as the one below.

## Gods on earth

The Egyptians believed that **pharaohs** were related to the sun god, Re, who was one of the most important gods. When a pharaoh started to rule, he started using a new name that included a set of special gods' names. This set often included the names of Re, Horus (the falcon god), and Nekhbet and Wadjet (the goddesses of Upper and Lower Egypt). Using the names showed that the gods would support and help the pharaoh.

# Queen Regent

When Tuthmosis II died, Egypt was again without a **pharaoh.** The people believed that the gods would be unhappy with this situation. They wanted a new leader.

### Tuthmosis III

Tuthmosis II and Hatshepsut did not have any sons. However, one of Tuthmosis II's other wives had a young son, Tuthmosis III. To become pharaoh, he would have to marry a royal princess, such as his half sister, Neferure.

Tuthmosis III was too young to marry or to rule. An adult would have to rule for him until he was older. This **regent** would have to make important decisions, so the job could not go to just anyone.

### Acting as ruler

Someone close to Tuthmosis III was perfect for the job—Hatshepsut. She learned a lot from her father, Tuthmosis I, and she may have even helped him rule. The law said that women could not become pharaohs, but it did not stop them from ruling as regents.

▲ Tuthmosis III, shown here in a wall sculpture, was not fully royal because his mother did not come from a royal family.

At first, Hatshepsut stayed in the background so that Tuthmosis III would be seen as the true pharaoh. But little by little, she took on more of the work and more of the power. She chose **officials** and **advisers,** and she made many decisions about running the kingdom. She also sent out the army when needed. Before long, Hatshepsut was basically ruling for herself, and Tuthmosis III held very little power.

▲ This painting from about 1500 B.C.E. shows traders traveling to Egypt. Hatshepsut communicated and traded with other nearby countries in Africa, Asia, and Europe.

### No power struggles

While Hatshepsut ruled as regent, Tuthmosis III was preparing to run the country as the next pharaoh. He learned about fighting battles and about pleasing the gods. Eventually, he was old enough and strong enough to make Hatshepsut give up power if he wanted to. However, he never forced her out. We may never know why he did not try to take power for himself when he could.

# A Female Pharaoh

As Hatshepsut gained power, she became more interested in ruling Egypt. Hatshepsut decided that she, not Tuthmosis III, would become the next **pharaoh**. However, some **historians** think that Hatshepsut planned to always include Tuthmosis III in important decisions.

### Wearing two crowns

Women had ruled Egypt before, but none had ever been pharaoh. In fact, there was not even an Egyptian word for a female ruler. So, Hatshepsut took the title of pharaoh.

Years earlier, Upper and Lower Egypt each had their own rulers. The king of Upper Egypt had a large, round white crown. The king of Lower Egypt had a tall red crown with a uraeus—a piece that looked like a snake—in front. Hatshepsut's crown combined parts of both crowns to show that she ruled all of Egypt.

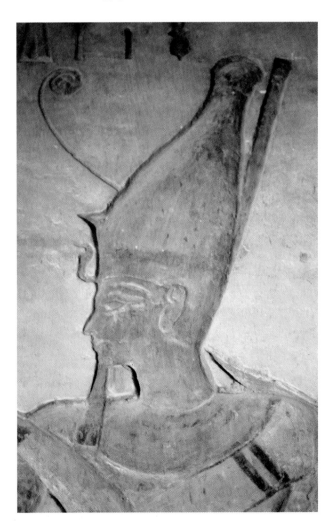

### Pharaoh in disguise

Hatshepsut worried that people would not accept a woman as their pharaoh. She wanted to follow **tradition** as much as possible. So she tried to make herself look like a man.

◀ Like Hatshepsut, Pharaoh Seti, shown here, wore the two crowns of Upper and Lower Egypt. Seti ruled Egypt years after Hatshepsut had died.

She shaved her head and wore short **kilts** instead of dresses. She even fastened a fake gold beard on her chin! People knew her as "His Majesty," just like any other pharaoh was known.

We have no way of knowing if Hatshepsut's changes tricked people. However, she did confuse historians. Sometimes, Hatshepsut appears as a man in paintings or carvings. Other times, she looks like a woman. **Archaeologists** once thought the images they found were of two different people. New discoveries of statues and other **artifacts** proved them wrong.

▼ This granite sphinx was built to show Hatshepsut's power. It is from about 1480 B.C.E.

### Sphinxes
A sphinx is an imaginary creature with a person's head on a lion's body. The message of a sphinx was that a ruler could protect his people. The lion stood for the pharaoh's power. The head was usually that of the ruler himself. Hatshepsut had many sphinxes made with her image for the head. She thought this would show how powerful she was.

# Close Advisers

Some people did not like Hatshepsut. They did not think a woman should be **pharaoh**. However, Hatshepsut did have a small group of trusted **advisers** who helped and protected her. They did not mind that she was a woman. She was a good leader, and her advisers became rich and powerful.

## Power and projects

Hatshepsut's advisers were involved in different groups. They helped strengthen Hatshepsut's power over everything that happened in Egypt. In return, Hatshepsut gave them jewels and other treasures. She praised them and gave them more important jobs.

One adviser named Hapuseneb helped with many of Hatshepsut's building projects. She gave him several important titles, including High **Priest** of Amen. This made him the head of all the priests in Egypt. Another man named Thuty kept careful records. Hatshepsut put him in charge of all her fortune. Thuty also designed beautiful decorations for many of Hatshepsut's building projects.

▶ This statue shows a scribe named Amenhotep. Hatshepsut's closest friend had studied as a young man to be a scribe.

## Senenmut

Hatshepsut's loyal advisers were also her dearest friends. Her closest and most powerful friend was Senenmut. He oversaw all the other men who served Hatshepsut.

Senenmut had grown up poor, but he learned to read and write so he could become a **scribe**. Hatshepsut hired him to teach her daughter, Neferure, which Senenmut thought of as being a great honor. He also designed and helped build Hatshepsut's great **temple**. Hatshepsut gave Senenmut many gifts, including two statues of him holding her daughter. Some **inscriptions** in Senenmut's **tomb** tell about Hatshepsut and her life.

▲ Hatshepsut gave Senenmut important jobs and more than 80 titles, such as **Steward** of Amen and Overseer of All Royal Works. Some of the titles can be seen in the writing on this statue of Senenmut.

### Senenmut's projects

Senenmut's work for Hatshepsut made him very rich. He also had some projects of his own. He had workers dig his own tomb right under Hatshepsut's. He chose a fancy **sarcophagus** for himself—something that only royal people usually did. Senenmut even carved his own picture in many places in Hatshepsut's tomb. Why did Hatshepsut let him do these things? Some **historians** think Hatshepsut and Senenmut may have been in love, but we cannot know for sure.

# A Beautiful Temple

Most of Hatshepsut's rule was peaceful, so she had plenty of time to work on projects in Egypt. She repaired many **temples** and other buildings that had been damaged in wars. She also had new buildings and statues constructed. The most important **monument** Hatshepsut's friends helped to build was her temple, which would later also contain her **tomb**.

### Hatshepsut's holy place

Most temples in Egypt were built to honor one or more gods. Hatshepsut dedicated her temple to the god Amen, who was the **divine** father of every **pharaoh.** Hatshepsut felt that Amen had brought her good luck. Hatshepsut wanted a place where she could praise and worship Amen.

Hatshepsut also planned to use the temple for her own tomb. When she died, she wanted to be buried there. Hatshepsut named the temple Djeser-Djeseru, meaning "Holy of Holies"—a blessed and wonderful place.

▶ Large sections of Djeser-Djeseru, Hatshepsut's temple, are still standing today.

## A wonderful design

Hatshepsut's temple does not look like most others built in Egypt around that time. **Historians** think that Senenmut designed her temple. Djeser-Djeseru was built into the side of a mountain at a place called Deir el-Bahri. It has three levels, with many columns supporting each level. The temple's design also included a garden with many plants—some from faraway lands.

Inside Hatshepsut's temple, paintings, carvings, and other decorations tell Hatshepsut's life story. They explain how she thought the gods chose her to be ruler. Some of the images show Hatshepsut as a girl or woman. Others show her as a boy or man. It is no wonder historians were confused!

▲ This painting is on one of the walls inside Hatshepsut's temple.

## Unsafe graves

Grave robbery was a huge problem in ancient Egypt. People sneaked into temples and tombs to steal the treasures inside. Hatshepsut was worried that someone might steal or harm her body after she died. Therefore, she built Djeser-Djeseru with several different burial rooms. As a result, no one would know which room actually held the real Hatshepsut.

# Trip of a Lifetime

Hatshepsut had another big dream. Since she was a child, she had heard stories of treasures from a faraway land called Punt. **Historians** think the land of Punt may have been located on Africa's southeastern coast, possibly near Somalia or Ethiopia. The Egyptians were not sure where the land was. Hatshepsut planned to send some ships there anyway.

## Riches from faraway

Hatshepsut thought that Punt had many riches that her people would want. Different traders sometimes brought items from Punt to Egypt. However, this took a long time. Hatshepsut hoped her sailors could find a way to sail to Punt so that she could trade directly with the people there.

Hatshepsut prepared five ships for the journey. Their crews included several of her **advisers** and some of her closest friends, including Senenmut. The sailors had no maps, and they also had no idea how far they would have to travel.

▲ The Egyptians were amazed to see people and treasures from the faraway land of Punt. This wall sculpture inside Hatshepsut's temple shows the queen of Punt in the center.

## An impossible journey?

The ships set sail from the city of Thebes, headed for the Red Sea. After that, no one knows where they went. Hatshepsut waited for the ships to return. Then, one day, she heard that the ships were coming. They had been gone for two years!

The whole city came out to watch. The ships were filled with amazing treasures. There were different kinds of perfumes, and valuable things like ivory, silver, and lots of gold. There

▲ This Egyptian artwork shows the Egyptian god Amen-Re protecting Hatshepsut. Hatshepsut wanted to please Amen-Re so he would treat her people well.

were also many live animals, including monkeys and giraffes. A few people from Punt even came along. One of the best things was a group of live trees, including 31 **myrrh** trees. Hatshepsut planted the myrrh trees in the garden of her **temple.** She also recorded many scenes from the trip on the temple's walls.

### The land of Punt

Punt was thought to be the home of Amen-Re, a god who had features of both the gods Amen and Re. Amen-Re later became known as the king of the gods. Hatshepsut hoped this journey to Punt would honor Amen-Re. She also wanted to bring some of Punt's treasures back to Egypt.

23

# A Year of Jubilee

Hatshepsut was pleased with her accomplishments. She decided to celebrate a year of jubilee, which is a time of special celebration. Most **pharaohs** held jubilees after ruling for 30 years. However, Hatshepsut's jubilee marked her fifteenth year as a ruler of Egypt. **Historians** are not sure why she chose to celebrate so much sooner than usual.

▲ One of Hatshepsut's tall obelisks is still standing. It can be seen in Egypt today.

### Making plans

Hatshepsut wanted to mark her jubilee by doing something important, but she also wanted to honor the god Amen. She already prayed to Amen daily and offered gifts at his **temple**. She had dedicated her own temple and other **shrines** to Amen as well. Finally, Hatshepsut decided to put up two grand **obelisks**. These tall towers would reach far into the sky.

## Building the obelisks

Hatshepsut put Senenmut in charge of the obelisks. At a **quarry** near the city of Aswan, his workers carefully removed a huge section of rock. The first piece cracked as they moved it, so they removed another section. The two huge pieces of rock were each almost 100 feet (30 meters) long. Each weighed thousands of pounds. The workers dragged the rocks to the Nile River nearby. They laid them on **barges** and floated them about 150 miles (240 kilometers) north to Thebes. It was hard to keep the barges from sinking or tipping over.

Obelisks were usually put outside buildings, but Hatshepsut wanted these to go inside the Great Temple of Amen. Workers had to remove the roof so the tall towers would fit. Hatshepsut wanted to cover both obelisks in gold, but this cost too much. So, she ended up coating just the tips with electrum, a mixture of silver and gold.

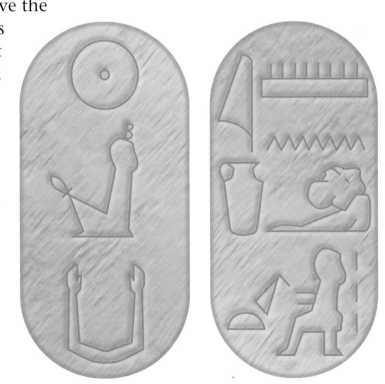

▶ This is Hatshepsut's cartouche, which is her name written in hieroglyphics and enclosed in ovals.

### Hieroglyphic writing

Hatshepsut's obelisks are covered with **inscriptions.** Most of these writings praise Amen, other gods, and Hatshepsut herself. **Hieroglyphics** is a kind of picture writing. Most of the pictures stand for objects, sounds, or ideas.

# Pharaoh No Longer

Like most ancient Egyptians, Hatshepsut spent a lot of time preparing for her death. She built her grand **temple** and filled it with rich treasures. She also had several fancy **sarcophagi** built for herself. Hatshepsut did not want grave robbers to disturb her **tomb** after she was buried. So, she tried to make it well-hidden and very hard to get to.

## *Hatshepsut's death*

No one knows exactly when or how Hatshepsut died. **Inscriptions** from her time offer some clues. For example, Hatshepsut's name suddenly stops appearing, and Tuthmosis III's name begins to appear more often—usually as the country's ruler. Therefore, Hatshepsut was probably dead.

People have two main ideas about how Hatshepsut died. One is that she simply got old. She probably reached her 40s or early 50s—fairly old for ancient Egyptians.

▶ This statue shows Tuthmosis III, who ruled Egypt after Hatshepsut died or was killed.

She may also have been killed by an enemy. Some **historians** think Tuthmosis III had Hatshepsut killed so he could finally rule for himself. We may never know the real truth. Hatshepsut's tomb is empty, and her mummy has never been found.

### After Hatshepsut

Tuthmosis III followed Hatshepsut as ruler of Egypt. Unlike Hatshepsut, he was not interested in peace. His armies made the **empire** larger by taking over other lands. Tuthmosis III became one of the strongest leaders Egypt ever had.

▲ Some pictures and writings about Hatshepsut were carefully scratched out.

About twenty years after Hatshepsut's death, someone tried to remove her name from history. **Archaeologists** have found her statues broken and her name and face scratched out of inscriptions. Even the royal records were changed to make it seem that she had never been **pharaoh**. It was as if she had never existed.

### Who destroyed Hatshepsut's records?

Historians are not sure who removed Hatshepsut's name from all these records. Some guess it might have been Tuthmosis III. In some places, his name was carved where Hatshepsut's name was removed. It could also have been others who did not think a woman should be pharaoh. They might have been trying to remove her name from history.

# Hatshepsut Lives On

Whoever tried to erase Hatshepsut from history was not completely successful. **Historians** first learned about her in the 1800s. At that time, Jean-François Champollion, the French historian and expert on Egypt, found some **inscriptions** about a king named Maatkare Hatshepsut. He knew how to figure out some **hieroglyphic** writing. However, some records said the king was male, and some said female. Champollion guessed wrongly that Hatshepsut had been a man.

Historians were confused for many years because none of the inscriptions about Hatshepsut seemed to make sense. The inscriptions did not always match with what was then known about Egyptian history.

◄ Historians understood Egyptian hieroglyphics better after the Rosetta stone, seen at left, was discovered. Greek writing on the stone explained what the hieroglyphics meant.

### Mummy mysteries

Hatshepsut's **temple** was partly buried in a landslide many years ago. In the early 1900s, a man named Howard Carter found **sarcophagi** that were made for Hatshepsut and her father, Tuthmosis I. However, there were no mummies inside the sarcophagi.

### Solving the puzzles

Finally, in the 1920s, **archaeologists** found something that explained a lot about Hatshepsut's life. It was an ancient garbage pit full of broken pieces of old statues. As scientists fit the statue pieces together, they learned new information about Hatshepsut and her life.

### Remembering Hatshepsut

We may never know Hatshepsut's entire story. Under her rule, Egypt enjoyed peace and grew strong. She expanded trade with other countries, including Punt. Hatshepsut also organized many grand building projects, such as her temple at Deir el-Bahri and the two **obelisks** in the Great Temple of Amen. One of these obelisks is the tallest standing obelisk in Egypt.

▲ This sculpture shows Hatshepsut wearing a crown. Her mummy may be destroyed, lost, or undiscovered.

Someday we may know more about Hatshepsut, a strong woman who did many great things. Most importantly, she dared to do what she was told she could not do. She made herself the first female **pharaoh** of Egypt.

# Glossary

**adviser** person who gives help or advice

**archaeologist** person who finds out about the past by studying the remains of buildings and other objects

**artifact** object that was made or used by humans in the past

**barge** flat-bottomed boat

**chariot** light cart with two wheels, pulled by horses

**divine** godlike

**embalmer** person who treats a dead body to keep it from decaying

**empire** large land or group of lands ruled by one person or government

**festival** special time of celebration

**hieroglyphic** any symbol used in the picture writing of ancient Egypt

**historian** person who studies and writes about the past

**inscription** words carved into a solid surface

**kilt** skirtlike garment

**linen** cloth made from the woven fibers of the flax plant

**monument** building or statue built to remind people of a famous person or an important event

**myrrh** sweet-smelling substance from a plant, sometimes used in perfumes

**noble** of high birth or rank in society

**obelisk** tall, four-sided post that narrows to a point at the top

**official** person who holds a position in a government or some other organization

**pharaoh** ruler of Egypt

**priest** person who performs religious rites or ceremonies

**quarry** place set up for digging stone from the ground

**regent** person who rules in place of a king or pharaoh

**ruin** remains of something, such as a building, that was destroyed

**sarcophagus** stone coffin, often with other coffins inside it. Two or more are called sarcophagi.

**scribe** person trained to write. Scribes often wrote government records and letters for other people.

**shrine** holy place, or a container with doors, inside which a god's statue or a royal coffin was kept

**steward** manager of a large organization or estate

**temple** building in which people worship a god or gods

**tomb** burial place, often marked by a stone or building

**tradition** usual pattern of thinking or doing things

# Time Line

| | |
|---|---|
| 3100 B.C.E. | King Menes is first to rule all of Egypt |
| | **Hieroglyphic** writing begins to be used to record history |
| 2686–2181 B.C.E. | Great Pyramids built |
| 1504–1492 B.C.E. | Tuthmosis I rules Egypt |
| about 1500 B.C.E. | Hatshepsut is born |
| 1492–1479 B.C.E. | Tuthmosis II rules Egypt |
| 1479–1473 B.C.E. | Hatshepsut serves as **regent** for Tuthmosis III |
| 1479–1464 B.C.E. | Hatshepsut's **temple** is built |
| 1473–1458 B.C.E. | Hatshepsut rules Egypt as **pharaoh** |
| 1458–1425 B.C.E. | Tuthmosis III rules alone |

# Pronunciation Guide

| Word | You say |
|---|---|
| Amen-Re | AH-men-RAY |
| Deir el-Bahri | day-EER el-BAH-ree |
| Djeser-Djeseru | JAY-sair jay-SAIR-oo |
| Hatshepsut | hat-SHEP-soot |
| hieroglyphic | HIGH-ro-GLIF-ik |
| Maatkare | maht-KAH-ray |
| myrrh | MURR |
| Neferure | NEF-er-oo-ray |
| obelisk | AH-buh-lisk |
| pharaoh | FAIR-oh |
| sarcophagus | sar-KOFF-uh-gus |
| sphinx | SFINGKS |
| Tuthmosis | TOOTH-mo-sis |
| uraeus | you-RAY-us |

# More Books to Read

Andronik, Catherine M. *Hatshepsut: His Majesty, Herself.* New York: Atheneum Books for Young Readers, 2001.

Malam, John. *Ancient Egyptian Women.* Chicago: Heinemann Library, 2003.

Shuter, Jane. *The Ancient Egyptians.* Chicago: Heinemann Library, 1998.

Shuter, Jane. *Pharaohs & Priests.* Chicago: Heinemann Library, 1999.

# Index

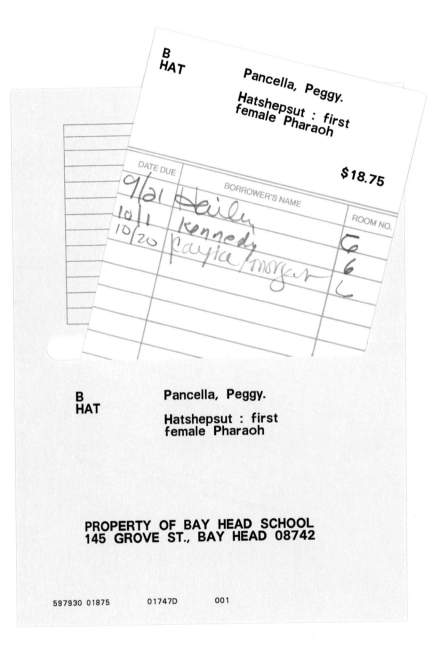

B
HAT

Pancella, Peggy.

Hatshepsut : first
female Pharaoh